HOW THIS BOOK CAME ABOUT

A few years ago I took a Feldenkrais class in Santa Cruz with Larry Goldfarb, founder of Mind in Motion. Toward the end of class, he said, "If I ever wrote a children's book, it would be called 'The Floor is your friend.'" I rushed home after class to my art studio and sketched out this book.

--Shelly Errington

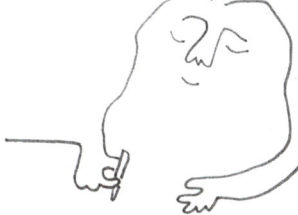

THE FLOOR is YOUR FRIEND

Copyright © 2025 by Shelly Errington

All rights reserved. No part of this book may be reproduced in any form or by any electronic or mechanical means including information storage and retrieval systems, without permission in writing from the author.

Printed in the United States of America
ISBN: 978-1-952194-44-3

Additional copies available from:
ShellyErrington.com
RiverSanctuaryPublishing.com
Amazon.com

River Sanctuary Publishing
Felton, California

THE FLOOR is YOUR FRIEND

a children's book for adults

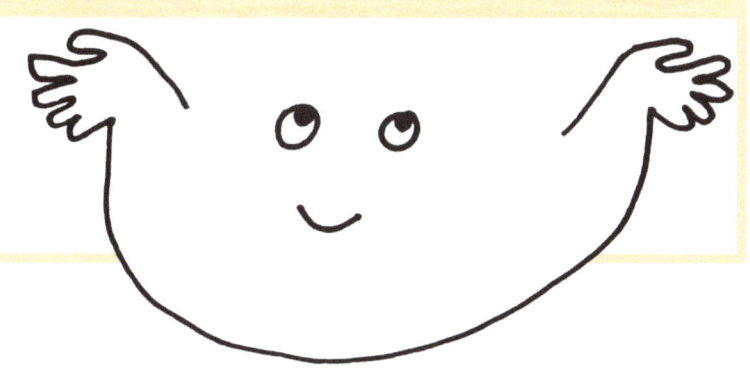

Shelly Errington

The floor has an even and undemanding temperament.

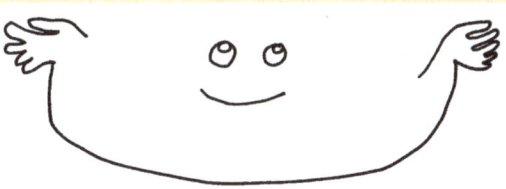

Its only agenda
is to support you

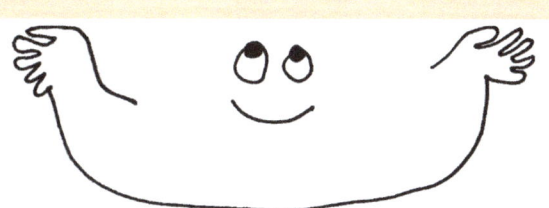

The floor's support is unconditional,
so you can relax completely
when you have a close relationship to it.

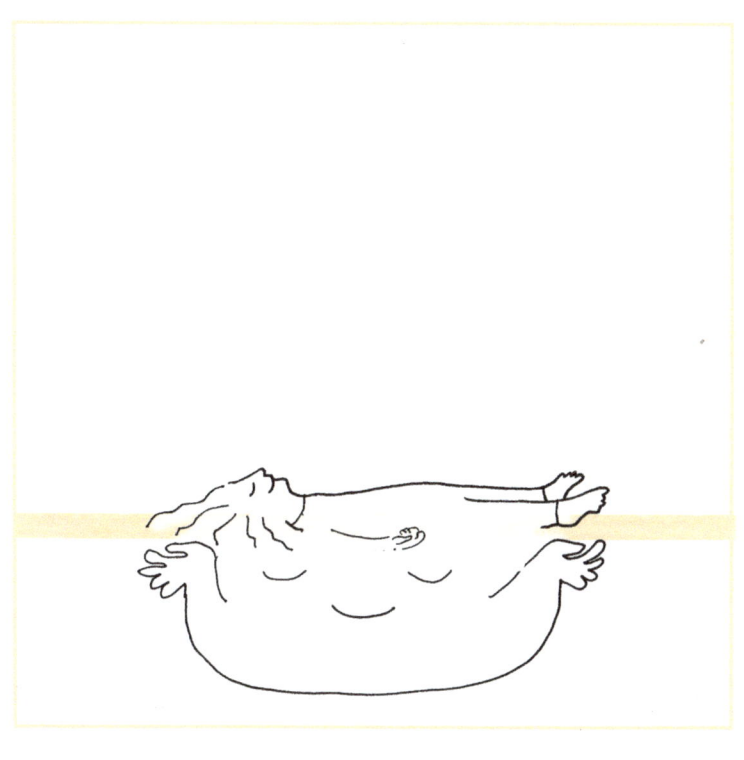

But the floor has clear boundaries,
so it will never try to hold on
when you need to take a break from it.

"That was really lovely, but I've gotta go to work now—"

The floor orients you in space
so you know
where up and down are.

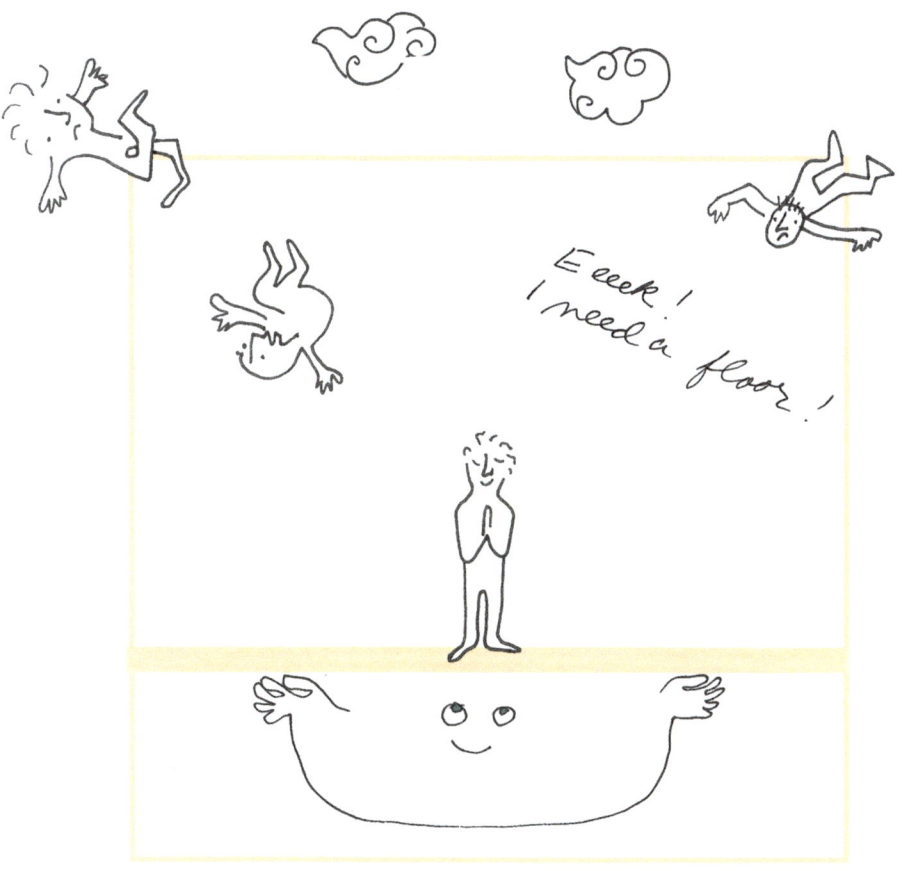

The floor cooperates with gravity
to hold down one end
so that the other end can
stretch up to the sky.

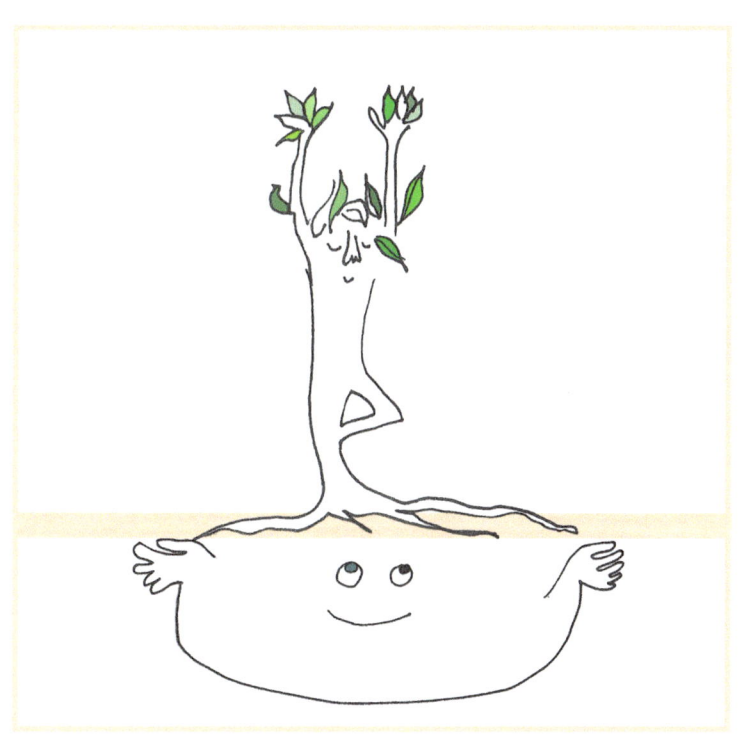

The floor never gets tipsy,
except on a cruise.

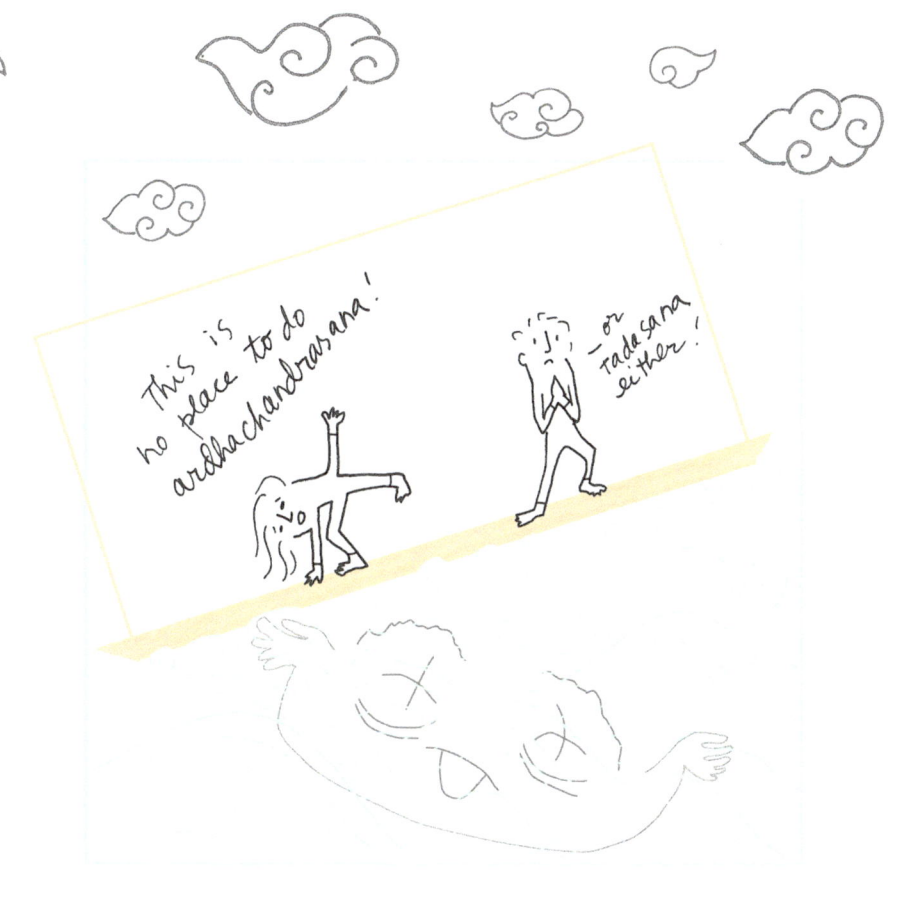

Although it gets stepped on a lot,
the floor seldom complains.

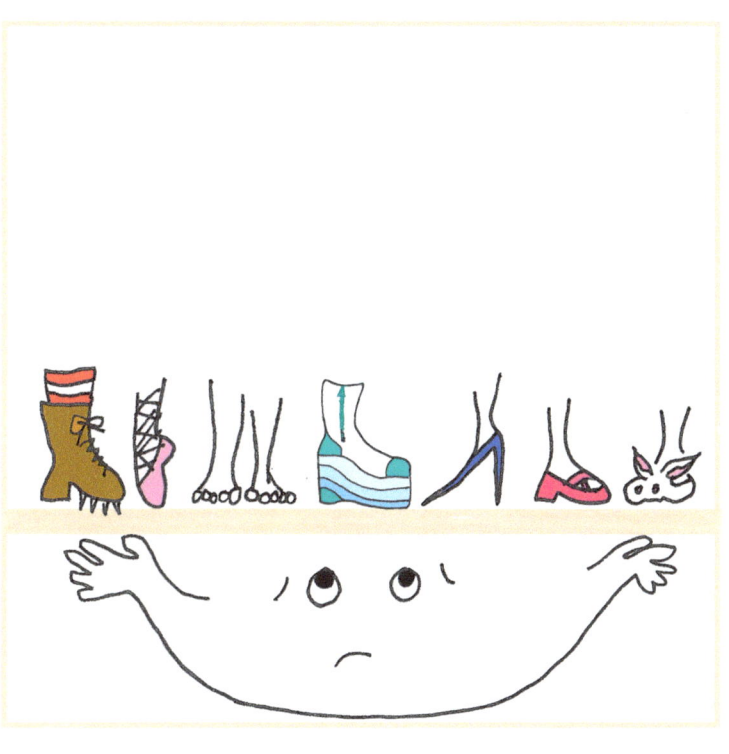

Some floors are high maintenance
on the surface,
but their underlying character
is still solid and dependable.

"I don't want a trophy floor!"

"I want a more easy-going relationship!"

HARDWOOD
FLUFFY WHITE CARPET
PARQUET

The floor doesn't mind

if you try new surfaces.

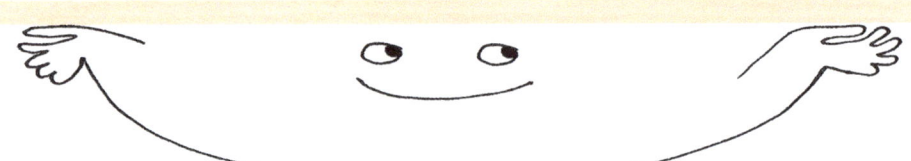

It will be waiting for you when you come back to it.

I realize it can be rough going out there but I wanna try it!

www.ingramcontent.com/pod-product-compliance
Lightning Source LLC
Chambersburg PA
CBHW051839210526
45473CB00005B/1939